Mountains

Roy Woodcock

Macdonald Educational

Contents

How to use this book
This book tells you about mountains. It describes how they are formed and looks at the main mountain ranges in the world. It also gives examples of animal and vegetable life found high up in mountains. Look first at the contents page to see if the subject you want is listed. For instance, if you want to find out about volcanoes, you will find that they are described on pages 12 and 13. The index will tell you how many times a particular subject is mentioned, and whether there is a picture of it. Mountain climbing, for example, is to be found on page 40. The glossary explains the more difficult terms.

A mystery explained

It is easy to understand why mountains have always been thought of as mysterious places. Capped in snow, cloaked in mist and cloud, and soaring high above the plains, it is not surprising that people believed that mountains were the homes of gods and spirits.

The ancient Greeks believed that Mount Olympus was the home of their gods and, today, some followers of the Shinto faith in Japan still hold Mount Fuji to be sacred.

Myth

Early man was always looking for explanations for things which puzzled him. Who made the Earth, the seas and the sky? He explained these things through stories. We call these stories myths. They

▲ Vulcan was the Roman god of fire. People believed that he worked as a blacksmith to the other gods. His forge was underneath Mt Etna, an active volcano in Sicily.

▲ Mt Fuji is in Japan. Followers of the Shinto religion believe it to be sacred. It is a perfect cone shape.

◄ Volcanic eruptions are a dramatic sight. This is a 19th century painting of lava flowing down on to the town of Portici from Vesuvius.

are full of creatures with superhuman powers, like gods and giants who could be held responsible for events which could be explained in no other way.

For example, a colourful explanation for a landslide of rock might have been giants or demons tearing lumps from the mountain peaks and hurling them at one another! And when a volcano erupted, it must have seemed as if the gods were at war with the human race.

The word volcano is taken from the name of one of the earliest Roman gods, Volcanus, later called Vulcan, the god of fire.

Science

Science has stripped away much of the old sense of mystery surrounding mountains. We now know why the Earth's surface is shaped as it is. The surface, or *crust*, is broken into huge sections, called *plates*. The plates are moving all the time but this movement is extremely slow; about one centimetre a year, ten kilometres over a period of a million years. Yet this is enough to make dramatic changes to the surface of the Earth. In many ways the facts of how a mountain is created are as strange and exciting as the old stories.

Our changing world

We think of the world as solid and unchangeable. In fact the surface is continually shifting; the continents are moving; mountains are being formed and being worn away; volcanic islands grow from the sea bed; even the oceans are changing in size and shape. These processes have been taking place over the millions of years since the Earth was formed.

Origins

About 4,600 million years ago the Earth solidified from gases and dust and became a sphere of rock. The centre of the Earth is called the *core*. This has remained extremely hot (probably about 3,000°C). The inner core is believed to be solid, the outer core liquid. Above the core is the *mantle*. The mantle consists of dense rock. But, near the top of the mantle, some rocks are molten, or liquid. This molten rock is called *magma*. If magma reaches the Earth's surface, it erupts in volcanoes.

Above the mantle is the Earth's crust. This is like a hard, light shell floating on the heavier mantle. The thickness of the Earth's crust varies. It is thinner beneath the ocean bed than the land masses. Its average depth is 25 km, though beneath high mountain chains it can be as deep as 70 km.

The plates

The Earth's crust is broken into large segments called plates. Currents, or movements, within the mantle cause the plates floating on the mantle to move as well.

INSIDE THE EARTH
The Earth has four layers: a solid inner core, a liquid outer core, the mantle and the crust. The mantle is mostly solid rock but parts of it are liquid. The crust floats on the mantle.

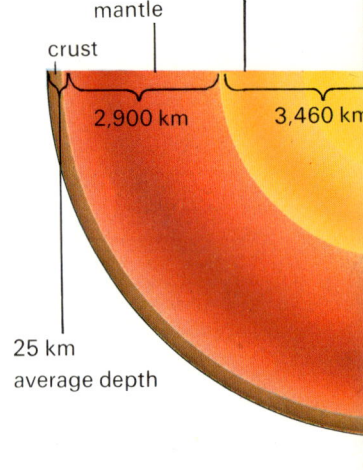

solid inner core
liquid outer core
mantle
crust
2,900 km   3,460 km
25 km average depth

Where the plates collide, new mountains can be pushed up, or crustal rocks can slide down beneath the neighbouring plate. This causes earthquakes. ▼

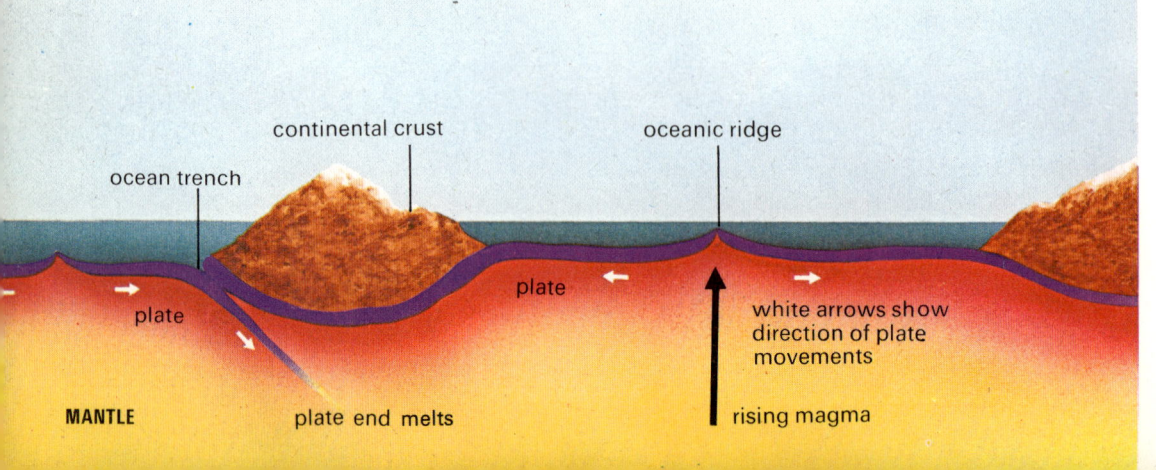

ocean trench
continental crust
oceanic ridge
plate
plate
white arrows show direction of plate movements
MANTLE
plate end melts
rising magma

Collisions

When the plates are forced against each other, a slow-motion collision takes place. Tremendous pressure grinds the plates together. The rocks between them are thrust upwards and huge mountain chains are formed. Beneath the sea there are mountain ranges. Here, where the crust is thinnest, magma comes to the surface forming new rock. The addition of this rock pushes the plates apart and so widens the oceans. In other places, one plate is pushed down beneath another. As this plate descends, it melts. Plate movements are not smooth. Most of the time, the plates are jammed together. Occasionally, they move suddenly and violently, causing earthquakes.

A full circle

Even as the mountains are rising, wind, rain, frost, ice and rivers begin to wear them away. Large and small rocks are broken off the mountains. These fragments are carried down to the sea by rivers or *glaciers* (masses of ice flowing down a valley). As they are moved, they are ground into even smaller pieces. Fine grains of rock are called *sediment* and this settles on lake or sea beds. Over millions of years, the sediment is compressed, or squashed to form new rocks. Plate movements might later thrust these *sedimentary rocks* upwards to form new mountain ranges.

The Earth's major plates can be seen on the map, and it is along these plate margins that most volcanoes and earth-quakes occur. ▼

•••• volcanoes
:::• earthquake zone

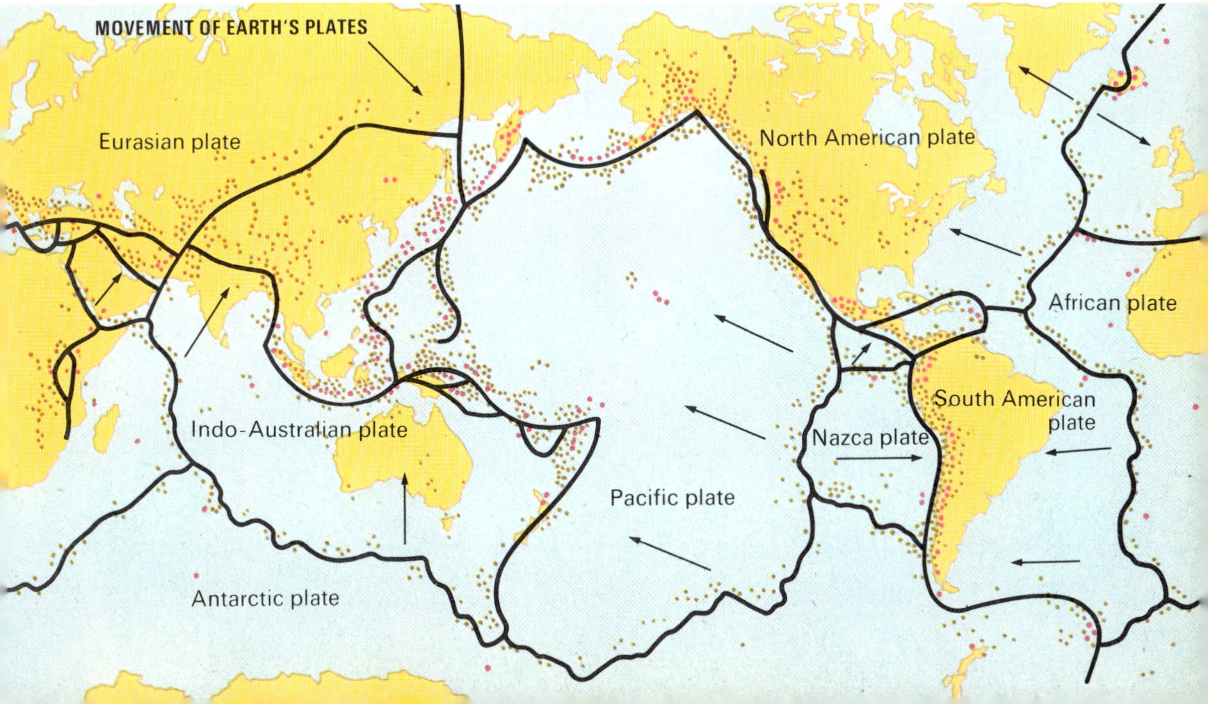

MOVEMENT OF EARTH'S PLATES

Eurasian plate

North American plate

African plate

Indo-Australian plate

Nazca plate

South American plate

Pacific plate

Antarctic plate

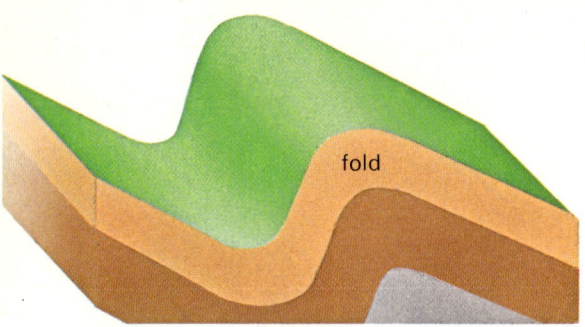

▲ If the layers of rock (strata) are affected by pressure from the sides, or underneath, they may bend. This is called folding. The diagram shows that great pressure from the right has made the fold lopsided.

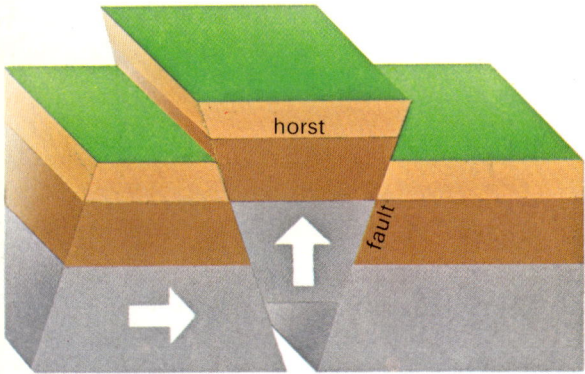

▲ Rocks may crack instead of bending when they are subjected to pressure. This is called faulting. If the pressure squeezes up a mass of land, this is called a horst or a block mountain.

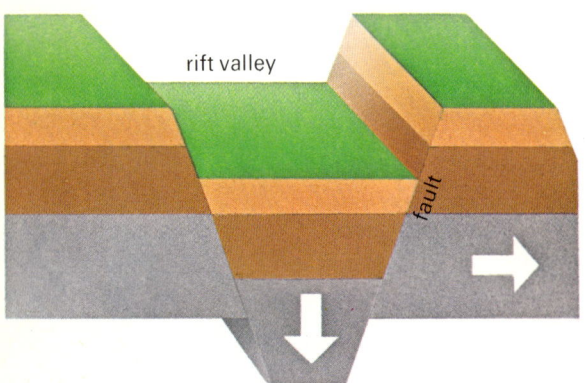

▲ The rocks between faults may slip down to form a rift valley. The sharp angles and corners in these diagrams are eventually rounded off by weathering, and they do not really look as steep in real life.

Formation of ranges

When two plates collide, great thicknesses of rock may be squashed together. As they are squeezed they *fold* or are *faulted*, which means they either bend or crack. Plate movement also causes some oceans to widen and others to shrink.

What was the Tethys?

There used to be a large ocean called the Tethys situated where the Mediterranean Sea is today. The Tethys covered a much larger area than the Mediterranean does now. As the African and European plates moved together about 80-100 million years ago, the Tethys Sea shrank. The Alps, Pyrenees and Atlas mountains were eventually all formed by the collision of these plates.

Evidence that these sedimentary rocks were once on the sea bed can be seen by studying fossil relics of animals embedded in rock. When these animals died, their remains fell to the sea bed. They were covered in sediment and gradually became part of the rocks. Their shapes can still be seen in the rock. Coral will grow only in the sea, but some fossilized coral has been found in the Pennine chain of northern England. This shows that the rocks that make up the Pennines were formed on the bed of a tropical sea, about 300 million years ago.

Rocks may crack

Faulting means that layers of rock have cracked, or fractured. Land between two faults may be pushed up to form high ground, or may slip down to form a large valley. A large valley formed by

fold mountains

remains of
ancient volcano

Rounded dome-shaped hills
are normally the result of magma
below the surface pushing up
the top layers of rock.

fault-block mountains

dome mountain

▲ This picture shows the four main types of mountain.

Lake Kivu is part of a chain of lakes in the African Rift Valley. ▼

land sinking between faults is called a rift valley. The East African Rift Valley is the world's largest. It contains a chain of lakes. Both Lake Malawi (also known as Lake Nyasa) and Lake Tanganyika are part of this chain. Loch Ness in central Scotland is in a small rift.

The land raised between faults is called a *horst*, or block mountain, and some of the highland areas in East Africa are horsts as are the Vosges in France.

Plateaux

Many horsts are quite flat, like tables, and do not have sharp pointed summits. Flat-topped highlands are called *plateaux*, and may be as high as the Bolivian plateau, nearly 4,000 metres.

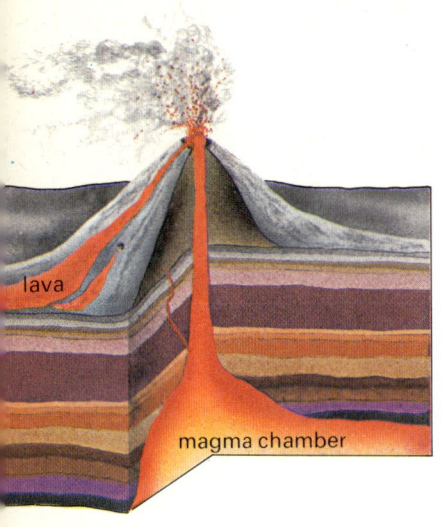

lava

magma chamber

Volcanoes

These are mountains which can be formed quickly when molten rock (magma) and cinders erupt through the Earth's surface. The movement may be dramatic and explosive, possibly blowing rocks and dust hundreds of metres into the air.

Types of volcanoes

Many volcanoes form from magma which comes from a melting plate edge. This happens when one plate is pushed down beneath another. Some volcanoes are very active and explosive, others are relatively quiet. When a volcano erupts violently, it means that the magma which has been building up beneath the surface is highly charged with explosive gases. A series of violent eruptions will build up a cone-shaped mountain. When there is not much gas in the magma, the volcano will erupt quietly. Quiet eruptions of fluid lava create shield volcanoes. These look rather like upturned saucers.

Active volcanoes

There are about 450 active land volcanoes in the world. This number may change since some volcanoes which

▲ Volcanoes often build up circular, cone-shaped mountains. This is because after each explosion a layer of ash and lava is deposited around the rim of the crater. Sometimes pressure in the main vent forces a vent to open in the side of the cone.
   Quiet eruptions of fluid lava create shield volcanoes.

◄ The lava is red hot underneath but cools and solidifies on the crust. The hot lava underneath keeps moving and so the crust is cracked and becomes rough and jagged.
   Lava may be sticky and slow moving or thinner and flow as fast as 20 km/h.

The black cinders and ash (tephra) thrown out by Helgafell, dropped on top of many of the houses and weighed down the roofs until some collapsed. The local people tried to keep sweeping off the tephra before the deposits became too heavy. ▶

we think are extinct may just be dormant. Dormant means that they have not erupted for several years, but could do so again.

Paricutin in Mexico first erupted in 1943. A peasant was working in his field when he felt tremors shaking the ground. Then he saw some smoke emerging from a hole further down the field. As the noise and smoke increased, solid matter was thrown up into the air and lava started to ooze out. Ash and lava piled up to a height of 400 metres over the next nine years. This volcano finally became dormant in 1952.

The most devastating volcanic eruption in modern times was at Krakatoa in 1883. Krakatoa is a small island volcano between Java and Sumatra in Indonesia. It had been dormant for 200 years before it exploded in 1883. Tsunamis, fast waves caused by the explosions, drowned over 30,000 people. One of the explosions was so loud it was heard in Australia, 5,000 km away.

Another well known volcano is Vesuvius which has erupted many times in the last 2,000 years, most recently in 1944. The most famous eruption was on 24 August AD 79. Within hours, the Roman town of Pompeii was buried under a thick layer of ash. In some places the ash was three and a half metres deep. The town has now been excavated and turned into a museum.

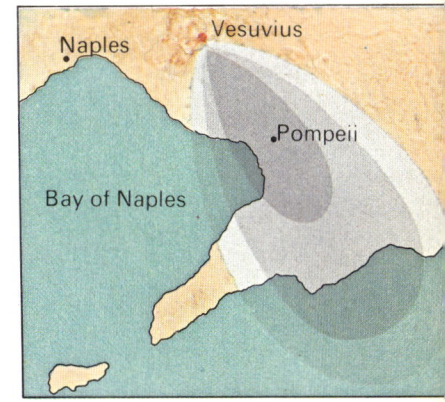

▲ The grey shadow shows the area affected by volcanic fallout from Vesuvius in AD 79.

Pompeii was buried under several metres of pumice and ash. ▼

Erosion

Mountains are constantly being worn away. This gradual process is called *erosion*. Sometimes mountains are eroded into flattish plains with occasional hills formed by hard, resistant rock. These are called *peneplains*.

Erosion

Erosion is the result of many things, including the freezing and thawing of water in the rocks. High mountains are affected by changes of temperature from day to night. Every night is cold in the mountains and the temperature may drop below freezing point. If water freezes it expands by about 9% of its volume. Water in cracks in the rocks freezes and expands at night and then melts during the day. This gradually shatters the rocks which explains why mountain peaks are very often jagged. The broken rocks tumble down hillsides and sometimes form piles called *scree*; sometimes they slide or are washed into rivers, which carry them away and break them into smaller and smaller pieces as they are swept downstream to the sea.

Rivers and ice

The world's landscape is continually changing. Erosion by rivers is responsible for much of this. The action of fast flowing water and of rocks being tumbled and scraped along the river bed deepens the river and eventually gouges steep-sided valleys in the mountains.

These mountains in Antarctica have been made rough and jagged by frost and ice action. ▼

▲ This is the kind of landscape seen in many Hollywood westerns. The mesas and buttes in the background are the isolated remains of plateaux.

However, the most dramatic changes in the northern *hemisphere's* landscape took place about two million years ago, during the last Ice Age. Ice from the mountains and the north, spread out across Canada and northern USA, and Scandinavia and northern Europe. We can still see the effects of this glacial erosion on the landscape today.

Glaciers

During the Ice Age, glaciers formed in the mountains and flowed downhill, following existing river valleys. The ice deepened and steepened the valleys to make them bigger and U-shaped. Many of these valleys have streams flowing into them from a great height and these form waterfalls. All the material eroded by the ice is carried downhill and eventually dumped at the sides of the valleys or out on the lowlands beyond the mountains. Some of this forms fertile soil and rich farmland.

The end of the mountains

Eventually, as a result of ice, water and frost, the old mountains will be worn down to peneplains and only isolated, steep-sided hills will remain. These isolated hills are called *inselbergen*, meaning island mountains. *Mesas* and *buttes* are the stark remains of eroded plateaux. They form a typical background to many of the western films shot in the southwest USA.

Mountains and man

The course of a country's history is often affected by the presence of natural barriers like mountain ranges, rivers and seas. One of the reasons Britain has remained independent for nearly a thousand years is because it is an island. On the other hand, Poland which is largely flat and has no natural boundaries has been invaded many times. Of course, to a determined invader almost any obstacle can be overcome.

Italy is separated from the mainland of Europe by the Alps. In former centuries, crossing these mountains in winter was almost impossible. Hannibal nearly conquered the Romans by managing to do just this; but he lost about half his army during the crossing.

Even with modern methods of transport, many parts of the world remain remote and difficult to reach. Some of the tribes living high up in the mountain valleys of Papua New Guinea have had no contact with the modern world at all and still lead a stone age way of life.

Mountainous regions also provide perfect hide-outs for bandits as well as strongholds for guerrilla armies, like those of the Kurds up in the mountains of Kurdistan in Iran. Today, there are still places like parts of Afghanistan or Sardinia which can be dangerous for travellers.

Hannibal's journey took him from Spain, through France and across the Alps. He believed this to be a better route to Rome than across the sea, which was controlled by the Roman navy.

Mountain settlements

Why should anyone choose to live in a mountainous area since such places are often remote and inhospitable? One explanation is that people may have sought refuge there when they were driven away from their homes in the lowlands by invaders.

Highland settlements also develop where minerals are found but these will only last for as long as the mineral is mined. Some people have deliberately sought the peace and seclusion from the outside world that mountains offer. Perhaps this is why certain religious orders have chosen to build monasteries in remote, mountainous areas.

Weather

In northern latitudes mountain life can be harsh.

In tropical latitudes some areas might be more pleasant than the surrounding lowlands. They are

▲ This pinnacle of rock, known as a puy, is the lava left in the neck of a volcano the outside of which has been eroded.

▲ When the Romans invaded Britain, many of the Celtic tribes were forced to retreat to the forests or mountains. Then they were able to hide and use their knowledge of the area to their advantage. Present day guerrillas still use the same tactics.

◀ Europeans working in India and Pakistan often holiday up in the hills to escape the hot summer weather. This picture, taken in 1896, shows a cricket match being played in Kohat, a town in the highlands of what is now Pakistan.

cooler and may contain better farmland. For example, the Tibesti range in the middle of the Sahara is surrounded by desert, but these mountains receive a little rainfall and so people can live there. In India there were hill stations such as Darjeeling where the families of the British officers could go to escape the excessive heat of the Indian summer. European people in India still go to the mountains, such as those in Kashmir, to get away from the hottest summer weather.

Mountain people

People, such as the Andean Indians, who live in high mountains all the time develop large lungs and wide nostrils. In this way the body can obtain more oxygen from the rarefied atmosphere. Rarefied means that the atmosphere is thinner and contains less oxygen. When lowland people go up to highlands, they cannot get enough oxygen and they puff and pant until they have become acclimatized (used to the thin air). Some athletes collapsed in the 1968 Olympics which took place in Mexico City—a city 2,240 metres above sea level.

Weather

Even in Britain, where the mountains are not very high, they do have a considerable effect on the weather.

Rainfall

Rainfall is heavier in mountains in Europe than in the lowlands. This is because the moist winds from the sea are forced to rise to pass over high ground. As they rise, they are cooled and so drop some of their water as rain. The side of the hills facing the wind, or windward side, is wetter than the other, or leeward, side. The land on the leeward side is often called the *rain shadow*.

Winds

Moist air gains or loses heat slowly; dry air gains or loses heat quickly. Therefore a moist wind, slowly becoming cooler as it rises up one side of a mountain and then losing its moisture through rain, becomes a dry wind rapidly gaining heat as it descends the other side. On the eastern side of the Rockies this wind is called the chinook. In the Alps it is called the föhn. Both winds bring warmer weather.

Sunshine and shade

The angle of the sun affects different slopes of valleys. The sunny side is called *adret* and the shady side *ubac*. Cold air rolls downhill and so will accumulate in hollows. These are called frost hollows and may be very cold at night. This is why orchards and vineyards are situated on the slopes and not in the valley bottoms. Alpine settlements are normally just up one side of the valley and, if possible, they are on the adret side.

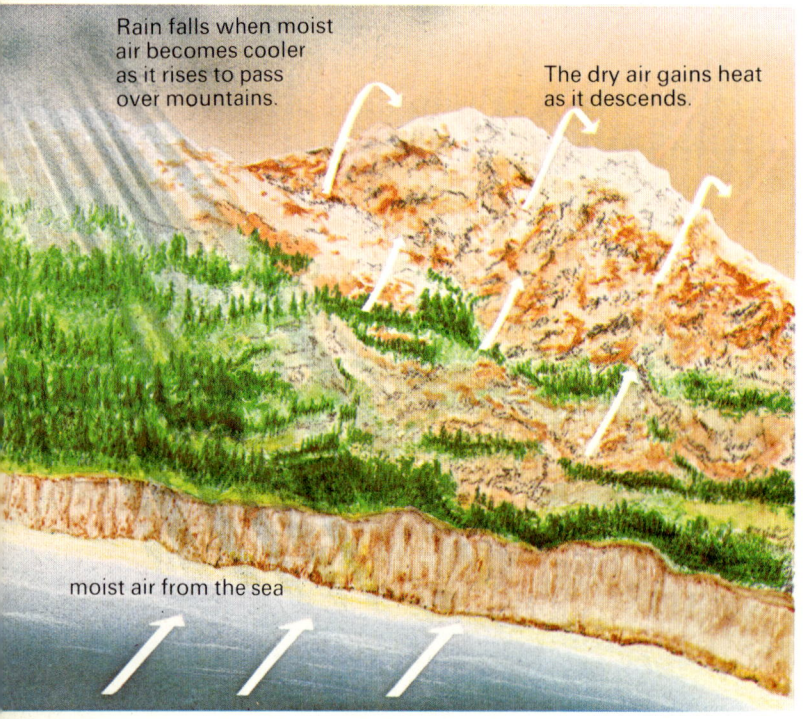

Rain falls when moist air becomes cooler as it rises to pass over mountains.

The dry air gains heat as it descends.

moist air from the sea

◄ The wetter, windward side of a mountain receives heavy rainfall and lush vegetation can grow there, as on the western slopes of the Sierra Nevada in California and the western Andes in southern Chile. The sheltered side of a mountain is much drier and has poorer vegetation. This side is called the rain shadow.

A small Alpine settlement perched on the adret, or sunny, side of the valley. ►

Cooler air

The higher you climb, the cooler it becomes, the temperature dropping by about 1°C for every 154 m. This is because the particles of dust and water vapour in the air, which retain warmth and control temperature, become fewer at higher altitudes. Therefore thinner mountain air can not absorb and retain the warmth from the Sun's rays. However the Sun's rays are very powerful at high altitudes and people skiing can become sunburnt even though the temperature is low.

Snow line

The *snow line* is the line on a mountain side above which there is always snow. This varies according to latitude and is over 5,000 m near the equator, and about 2,100 m in the Alps. It is at sea level in Antarctica.

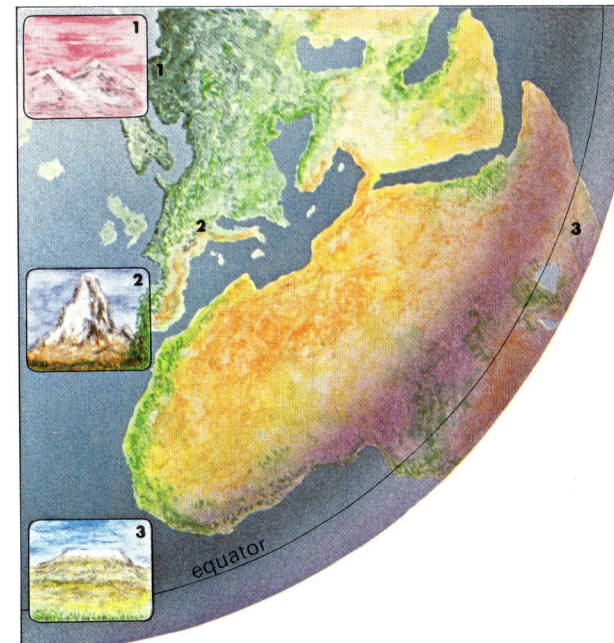

▲ 1 A mountain inside the Arctic Circle: the snow line is at sea level.
2 Matterhorn: in the Alps the snow line is at about 2,100 m.
3 Kilimanjaro: the snow line is over 5,000 m near the Equator.

Mountain vegetation

The higher up a mountain you climb, the colder it becomes. As the conditions change, so too does the vegetation. For example, at a certain height the conditions are such that trees are no longer able to grow. This is called the tree line. Flowers which grow between the tree line and the permanent snow are called alpines. Most of them are found in the alpine meadows, the area just above the tree line. Only mosses, lichens and the hardiest flowering plants survive higher than this.

Alpines tend to be small to avoid the full force of the wind. Long roots enable them to get a good grip on the soil and to absorb enough moisture. Leaves are either waxy like those of the glacier buttercup or hairy like the edelweiss. Hairy leaves trap heat and are a protection against the cold. Cushion-shaped plants like the moss campion have two advantages: their low, round shape is an ideal defence against wind, whilst the interior is a heat-trap, retaining the Sun's heat at night. Alpines have brightly coloured flowers which absorb light and heat and also attract the few insects found in the mountains.

The alpine soldanella can melt its way through snow by radiating stored energy as heat.

A number of alpine plants root themselves in tiny crevices in the bare rock. The name saxifrage means 'rock breaker'.

saxifraga crustata   primula hirsuta

glacier
buttercup

trumpet gentian

mountain aven

alpine
marguerite

edelweiss

alpine
butterwort

moss
campion

▲ These flowers
flourish in high, wet
places.

▲ The moss campion's
round shape protects it
from the wind.

▲ The edelweiss and the
gentian like dry, rocky
ground.

golden
eagle

Mountain wildlife

Mountain animals have to be adaptable and hardy in order to find food and survive the harsh weather.

Rocky Mountain goats and chamois are both more closely related to the antelope rather than the goat family. They are skilful climbers, feeding on lichens and grasses high up on the craggy cliff faces. The chamois was almost exterminated by hunters, but now it is a protected animal in the Alps. The Rocky Mountain goat rarely leaves the heights where it is safe from predators like the mountain lion. It has a thick winter coat which enables it to endure temperatures as low as minus 40°C.

Some animals like the marmot survive the cold by hibernating. Their breathing and heart beats slow down, enabling them to conserve heat and energy.

Of all animals, birds are probably the best adapted to high altitudes. Eagles and vultures can glide around the high peaks. Their sharp eyesight enables them to spot prey or carrion hundreds of metres below.

Some people believe that the yeti, or abominable snowman, lives in the Himalayas.

mountain
lion

marmot

The picture shows four types of mountain animal. The golden eagle nests high up in mountain cliffs, preying on small animals like the marmot. The mountain lion is another predator, hunting larger creatures like deer and elk. The Rocky Mountain goat is one of the most sure-footed climbers of all. It seeks out mosses, lichens and grasses up on the craggy cliff-faces of mountains. The marmot is a rodent. It survives the cold by hibernating in burrows and rock crevices during the winter months.

Rocky Mountain goats

The Himalayas

This is not the biggest or greatest mountain range in area or length, but does contain the world's highest mountains. The Himalayas are part of a vast mountain area which includes the Pamirs, Hindu Kush and Karakorams. Between the Himalayas and the Kunlun Shan range is the Tibet plateau which is more than 3,000 m above sea level. Mount Everest is on the border of Tibet and Nepal.

Water suppliers

These ranges of mountains are very important to India. Because of their size and height, they contain huge expanses of snow. Great glaciers feed several large rivers, notably the Ganges, Indus and Brahmaputra which help to irrigate land in India and Pakistan.

▲ The Himalayas separate the Indian sub-continent from the desert lands of Central Asia.

A party of Indians climbing up a Himalayan pass in winter. ▼

The summits

The three highest peaks are Everest (8,848 m high and named after a 19th century surveyor, Sir George Everest), K2 which is in the Karakorams (8,610 m) and Kangchenjunga (8,598 m).

Mount Everest

The approach to Everest is normally made through Nepal, although it has now been climbed from the Tibet side as well. Expeditions usually employ local people (the sherpas) as porters. Some of the sherpas have become very good mountaineers. Of course the local people are acclimatized to the rarefied (thinner) air, but even they cannot climb the great heights of the Himalayas at all easily.

There have been several successful ascents of Everest. The first was achieved on 29 May 1953 by a New Zealander, Sir Edmund Hillary, and Sherpa Tenzing. They were better equipped than earlier expeditions, carrying oxygen tanks to overcome the problem of the thin air.

The mountain has claimed many lives. A tragic and mysterious attempt on Everest took place in 1924. G Mallory and A Irvine set off for the summit on 8 June. They were seen entering cloud at about 8,540 m. No one knows whether they reached the summit or not.

Himalayan countries

The Himalayas stretch across four countries: India, Pakistan and the small kingdoms of Nepal and Bhutan. Sikkim was an independent kingdom but it became part of India in 1975. There are several groups of people living in Nepal. One of these groups, the Gurkhas, became dominant a few centuries ago.

▲ The mountain people in Asia work hard to make a living. The hill slopes are cut into terraces so that they can grow crops like wheat and rice.

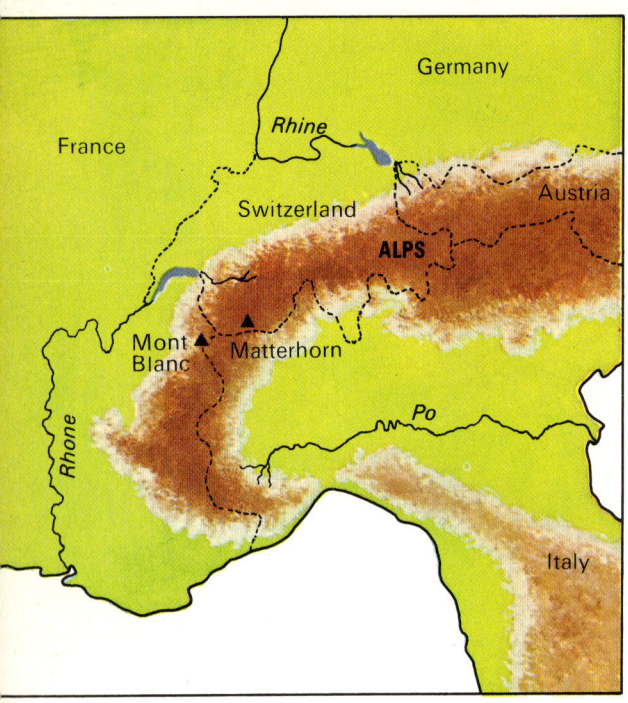

▲ The Alps extend through France, Italy, Switzerland and Austria. Tributaries of many major European rivers rise in the Alps

Grindelwald, a popular Alpine ski resort.▼

The Alps

These mountains extend from France, through Switzerland and Italy, into Austria. They contain many impressive peaks, the highest being Mont Blanc (4,807 m) on the Franco-Italian border. This is often said to be the highest mountain in Europe, but there are several peaks in the Caucasus Mountains, which extend from the Black Sea to the Caspian, which are higher.

Farming

The mountains are often forested at lower levels, with patches of grassland above the forest. These grasslands are known as *alpine pastures*.

The farmers grow crops in the valleys, notably hay and other cattle foods, but there are some orchards and vineyards on the slopes. In winter, cattle are normally kept in sheds attached to the houses so that they can be reached without going outside. In the summer, they are taken up to the alpine pastures. This is called *transhumance* farming. Some of the milk is made into cheese. Gruyere, Emmenthal and other varieties come from this area, and there are also chocolate-making firms using the surplus milk. The people may be involved in farming, but in winter when days are short, they may be snowed in.

The houses have overhanging roofs so that when snow falls off them it will not fall on to the windows or doorways. Beneath the overhang are piles of wood stored ready to be used as fuel, as each family collects wood all through the summer for use during the winter. Some houses have flattish roofs so that the snow forms an insulating layer. During the winter months some of the men work in the forestry industry.

Tourists

Tourists come throughout the year, but there are certain peak times. The winter snows attract skiers from Christmas until about Easter. Many of the best resorts are high up on the alpine pastures. Climbers come mostly in the summer. Hundreds of people climb the Matterhorn, but only a few climbers have managed to scale the north face of the Eiger which is very steep and difficult.

July and August are popular months for sightseeing. The narrow winding roads and also the mountain railways become rather crowded, often spoiling the peaceful atmosphere of these mountains.

Communications

Alpine people have overcome their geographical isolation by building roads and railways. In difficult places, zigzags and tunnels are used to overcome the steep mountain slopes. There are many passes which are used by cars in the summer, for example the Great St Bernard which links Italy with Switzerland, and the Brenner which links Austria with Italy. These passes are also used by the post buses which carry mail and passengers. However, many of the roads become impassable in winter and so the railways are much more important in the snowy weather. The trains are nearly all electric, which is useful as electric trains are better on steep slopes and there is much electricity available because of all the hydroelectric power schemes in the Alps.

▲ These mountains were forming about 25 million years ago when the African plate pushed smaller plates against Europe.

A small Alpine lake. Alpine plants can be seen in the foreground. ▼

Norwegian mountains

During the last Ice Age, Norway was covered by massive ice-sheets. Its rugged, mountainous landscape is largely the result of erosion which took place during this glacial period. The main mountain area is called the Jotunheimen. The highest peak is Galdhopiggen (2,469 m). In many places high mountains are close to the coast.

There are still glaciers on the mountains including the largest ice cap in mainland Europe, the Jostedalsbre. Evidence of former ice-action can be seen everywhere. Dramatic remnants of the Ice Age are the fjords.

Fjords

Fjords were formed by glaciers carving steep, U-shaped valleys. When the ice melted, the sea level rose and these valleys were flooded. Some of the largest are astonishingly deep—deep enough for a supertanker to sail up them.

The fjord valley often extends back into the mountains. In a few cases a small glacier can be seen at the head of the valley. Usually a river flows along the valley and into the fjord. Where river and fjord meet, a flat area of land is built up by the river dropping sediment there, creating a *delta*. This is usually the best farm land and is frequently the only place on the fjord where there is a village.

The people

Many of the people earn a living from fishing and farming. Like farmers in the Alps they are transhumance farmers. The cattle are kept indoors in the winter and are not taken up the mountain until the snows have melted from the alpine pastures. Several crops of hay are necessary to feed the cattle in winter.

This fjord is surrounded by steep-sided mountains. The calm, deep water makes a perfect natural harbour. A small village can be seen in the background. ▶

Houses are sometimes built into the hillside to protect them from falling stones. ▼

The Andes

The Andes are a series of mountain ranges linked together by basins and plateaux. For example, the three ranges in Colombia are separated by large river valleys. In Bolivia, Peru and Ecuador, the ranges are connected by plateaux. These are called *intermontane* plateaux and are between 3,500 and 4,000 m above sea level. Life is often harsh at these altitudes.

Indians

The local people are American Indians. They are mostly poor farmers growing crops for their own needs. Even so they do not always get enough food. The soil is thin and stony, and the weather is often bitterly cold. Potatoes and barley are the main crops. Llamas are very important: they are used as beasts of burden; they also provide milk and wool.

The most famous Indians in the past were the Incas. They developed an advanced civilization and built many fine buildings. They cut thousands of terraces into the steep hillsides so that crops could be grown. Their capital was at Cuzco on the Peruvian plateau. The Incas were overpowered by the Spanish invaders led by Francisco Pizarro in the 1530s. Pizarro founded the city of Lima down near the coast.

Minerals

The Incas were rich in silver and gold, but this was taken from them by the Spanish. There are still many mineral deposits in the Andes, notably tin and copper. Conditions are hard in the mines and the Indian workers are poorly paid.

▲ The Andes range extends the full length of South America. The Amazon rises in its foothills.

A Peruvian girl leads a llama. The llama's coat is an important source of wool. ▼

Lake Titicaca

Lake Titicaca is on the plateau between Peru and Bolivia and it is the world's highest lake with regular steamer navigation. One of the boats was taken up the mountain in pieces and assembled on the lake side. Some of the local Indians have reed boats, which their tribes have been making for centuries.

Roads and railways

It has been extremely difficult establishing links across the Andes, but some good roads are now being built. One of the most remarkable railways in the world goes inland from Lima, up into the Andes at Huancayo. In the 420 km there are 66 tunnels, 59 bridges and 22 zigzags, and the line reaches a height of 4,782 m. It was completed in 1893. It is a tremendous feat of engineering skill.

▲ Lake Titicaca is nearly four km above sea level. The local Indians make boats from reeds.

Macchu Picchu is a fine relic of the Inca civilization. ▼

The Rockies

The Rocky Mountains are a long range extending from northern Canada to southern USA. The mountains are close to the coast in the north, but are over 1,500 km inland in the south. They form the dividing line between the mountainous lands which extend to the Pacific coast, and the rolling plains of the prairies to the east.

The highest peak is Mount Elbert (4,399 m) in Colorado and the highest in Canada is Mount Robson (3,954 m). As with the Himalayas, the high ground is often snow-covered. *Meltwater*, together with rainfall, creates many rivers, such as the North Platte, Missouri and Colorado. These are important sources of water for irrigation to farmers on both sides of the Rockies. Because of the magnificent scenery, there are several national parks in the Rockies.

▲ This old Indian castle was the home of Chief Montezuma.

People

The Rockies were a tremendous obstacle to early settlers moving west. Many died of cold in the freezing weather high up in the mountain passes or were killed by the Indians. Some of the routes pioneered by the settlers were followed by railway builders. Construction teams were frequently attacked by Indians who resented the intruders coming into their homeland.

Some of the Indians, such as the Hopi, lived in cliff dwellings. They grew their crops down in the river valleys. Others, such as the Navajo, herded sheep on the plateaux.

Towns

There are some important towns at the foot of the Rockies, including Edmonton and Calgary in Canada, Denver and Colorado Springs, in Colorado. These towns are thriving, but many towns have declined. When valuable minerals like gold were discovered in the Rockies, towns grew up very quickly around the mines, but were abandoned just as quickly when the mineral ran out. Some old, empty towns may be seen in several places. These are called ghost towns.

▲ This is a restored ghost town in Nevada.

▲ The grizzly bear is found in the remote forest areas of North America.

The Rocky Mountain System extends from Alaska to Central America. ▶

A view of the Colorado Rockies. ▼

Australasia

Australasia includes Australia, New Zealand and many islands, the largest being Papua New Guinea. North Island, New Zealand has several volcanoes. South Island contains the Southern Alps where there are many glaciers. The highest point in Australia is Mount Kosciusko (2,230 m) in the Australian Alps. These are one of many ranges making up the Great Divide. Kosciusko was quite isolated until work began on the great Snowy River irrigation and hydro-electric power scheme, but no mountains in Australia are as isolated as some in Papua New Guinea. On this island there are groups of primitive people isolated from the outside world. This is because the high mountains and dense forests hinder travel and exploration. These tribes are even more isolated than the Australian Aborigines.

The Great Divide
The Great Divide in eastern Australia consists of many separate ranges such as the Blue Mountains and the New England Range. These mountains affect the climate of much of Australia. They keep the rain-bearing winds from travelling inland. The narrow strip of land to the east of the Great Divide is wet and productive, but the majority of Australia is to the west of these ranges and is dry because of the rain shadow effect.

The Snowy River scheme
There are many rivers which flow down the east side of the mountains, and one of these, the Snowy, has been dammed.

▲ Aborigines are the original inhabitants of Australia. They are a nomadic people.

Canberra, a planned city, is a complete contrast with the harsh outback where the Aborigines live. ▼

Much of its water now flows through channels and tunnels to join the rivers Murray and Murrumbidgee flowing west into the interior. The Snowy River scheme provides extra water for irrigation in the interior. Hydro-electricity is also produced in large quantities. Dams have been built and several large lakes have been formed. These are now used for boating and fishing. The roads which had to be built for the people working on this scheme are now used by skiers driving up to the snow around Mount Kosciusko.

Canberra

In the mountains not far from the Snowy River is Canberra, the capital of Australia. It was specially built as the capital in 1911. Sydney and Melbourne are Australia's two largest towns, and to avoid arguments a site was chosen for the capital half-way between them.

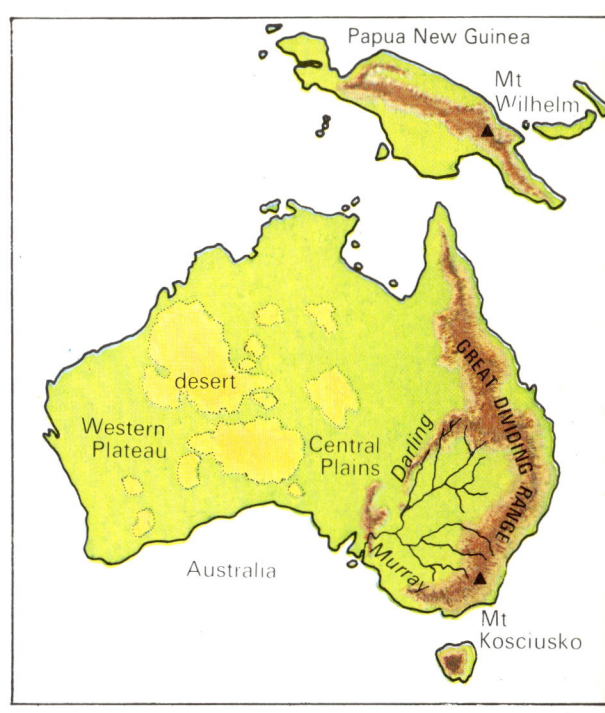

▲ The River Murray is fed by tributaries rising in the Australian Alps.

There are many small tribal groups living in the remote mountain valleys of Papua New Guinea. ▼

Island mountains

Many large mountains grow up from the sea bed and form islands which are volcanic in origin, such as the Hawaiian Islands. Some larger islands may also be formed by rocks squeezed up from the ocean bed.

All the Hawaiian islands are volcanic, though many of the volcanoes are now either dormant or extinct. They have formed many large mountains including one which receives over 11,250 mm of rainfall each year and is one of the wettest places in the world. The highest mountain is Mauna Kea (4,206 m). In fact more than half this mountain is below sea-level. Measured from the sea-bed it is taller than Everest.

The Canary Islands are all of volcanic origin, as are Tristan da Cunha and Ascension in the southern part of the Atlantic. Iceland, in the North Atlantic, is located on the mid-Atlantic Ridge. There has been much volcanic activity in Iceland in recent times. A major eruption occurred at Heimaey in 1973.

▲ The mid-oceanic ridge in the Atlantic is the largest mountain range in the world. It is an area of intense volcanic activity, because it is situated where two plates meet. All along the ridge, lava is breaking through and forming new rock.

▲ The Fire Mountain of Lanzarote, one of the Canary Islands, has many patches of hot rock on the surface. In some places it is so hot that twigs thrown on the ground will burst into flames.

◄ Surtsey is a new volcanic island off the coast of Iceland. It appeared above the waves in November 1963. The island then formed rapidly from the solidifying lava.
Iceland is actually part of the Atlantic mid-oceanic ridge. It is growing wider by about one centimetre a year because new rock is being formed all the time along the whole length of the ridge.

Steam was first seen coming out of the sea off the coast of Iceland by fishermen in November 1963. Eruptions of ash and then lava built up a small mountainous island called Surtsey. This has been studied and recorded since its birth. A careful watch is kept not only for volcanic activity, but also to record plants which have managed to grow on this black volcanic island.

Mediterranean volcanoes

There are several volcanic islands in the Mediterranean Sea, especially in the Lipari group just to the north of Sicily. The Liparis contain Vulcano and Stromboli, the latter being called the Lighthouse of the Mediterranean.

Farther east, off the coast of Greece, is the island of Thera. There was a massive explosion more than 3,400 years ago, and part of the island disappeared. The ash from Thera may have helped to destroy the Minoan civilization on Crete. It is possible that this island which partially disappeared gave rise to stories about the legendary lost continent of Atlantis.

Sports

There are many activities which can be enjoyed in mountainous areas. People can ski, climb, trek, canoe on the streams, as well as just admire the scenery. Of course, there is a danger that too many visitors could spoil the peace and beauty of mountains—the very qualities which attract people in the first place. Some countries have set up national parks where rare species of plant and wild life can be protected.

Skiing and climbing

People living in countries such as Norway needed to have a way of travelling across the snow. Skis were a solution to this problem. The first skis were long and thin, like those used for cross-country skiing today. They were designed more for gliding across the snow than for travelling fast downhill. Much of this kind of skiing takes place on flat or gently sloping ground. Downhill skiing can be fast and dangerous. The world record set in 1979 is 202 km/h.

Many children brought up in places like the Alps or Norway learn to ski at an early age. It is not surprising that those countries produce many good skiers.

Climbing ability was a necessity for some mountain people, especially for those who had to look after animals grazing up on the alpine pastures. Like skiing, it has now become a major sporting activity. A climber needs more than courage and a good head for heights. It is a highly skilful sport, requiring team work, knowledge of mountain conditions and good equipment.

▲ Even the most experienced climbers face great dangers when ascending steep, snow-covered rock walls.

Skiing in the Alps. ▶

Dangers

Mountains may be picturesque, but they must also be treated with respect and caution. Anyone visiting mountains should be well prepared for difficulties. A clear, sunny day can become cloudy, snowy or freezing within a few minutes. Even if the weather is fine at the bottom of the mountain, it will be much colder higher up. Strong boots and sensible waterproof clothing are essential. People die each year just because they are not prepared for a change in weather conditions. They also endanger the lives of those who have to form the rescue party.

Avalanches can build up to speeds of 110 km/h, flattening trees and houses standing in their way. ▶

Avalanches

In areas which receive heavy falls of snow, a warm autumn can signal the danger of avalanches later in the year. This is because the first fall of snow does not stick properly to the ground. During the course of the winter, as snow piles up higher and higher, the ground layer of snow starts to slip. What is at first just a small movement can turn into a huge and very dangerous avalanche.

Avalanche fences and sometimes coniferous forests are situated above a village as protection; though a large and powerful avalanche will sweep everything aside.

In the Alps there are special avalanche

rescue teams. They use long poles and specially trained dogs to try and locate anyone buried under the snow. Most people buried by an avalanche will die quite quickly, but there are stories of people living for hours, until rescued.

Acclimatization

Another danger in very high mountains is *soroche*, or mountain sickness. It is important for people from low levels to acclimatize themselves quite slowly if, for example, they are climbing in the Himalayas or the Andes. Anyone climbing too quickly may become sick and could suffer brain damage through lack of oxygen.

Communications

All mountains present a hazard to flying as well as to other types of travel. Snow and ice on the road can make driving very dangerous. Railway lines can become blocked from falls of rock or snow. Particularly vulnerable places are sometimes covered over by a roof for protection.

Books to read

Earthquakes, Volcanoes and Mountains, Macdonald Colour Unit 1971
Rocks and the Landscape, Macdonald Colour Unit 1972
Snowdonia National Park Scenery, National Museum of Wales 1977
Mountainous Landscapes, M. J. Smith; Jacaranda Press 1967
The Observer's Book of Geology, I. O. Evans; Frederick Warne 1971
The Rocky Mountains, B. Walker; Time Life Books 1974
South American Handbook, Trade and Travel Publications (annual)
Soviet Deserts and Mountains, Time Life 1975
The Next Horizon, C. Bonnington; Arrow 1973
Everest The Hard Way, C. Bonnington; Arrow 1976

Things to do

You can make models of mountains in plasticine or with papier maché. Models can also be made from cardboard if a map with contours is available. Trace round each contour and cut out a piece of cardboard to match the shape of the contour. If you then place the pieces of cardboard on top of each other, the shape of your model will be the same as the hill.

The world's main ranges

1	Rockies			13	Tien Shan
2	Appalachians			14	Kunlun Shan
3	Andes	8	Drakensberg Mountains	15	Himalayas
4	Scandinavian Mountains	9	Elburz Mountains	16	Great Dividing Range
5	Alps	10	Urals	17	Southern Alps
6	Pyrenees	11	Hindu Kush	18	Carpathians
7	Atlas Mountains	12	Pamir Knot	19	Caucasus Mountains

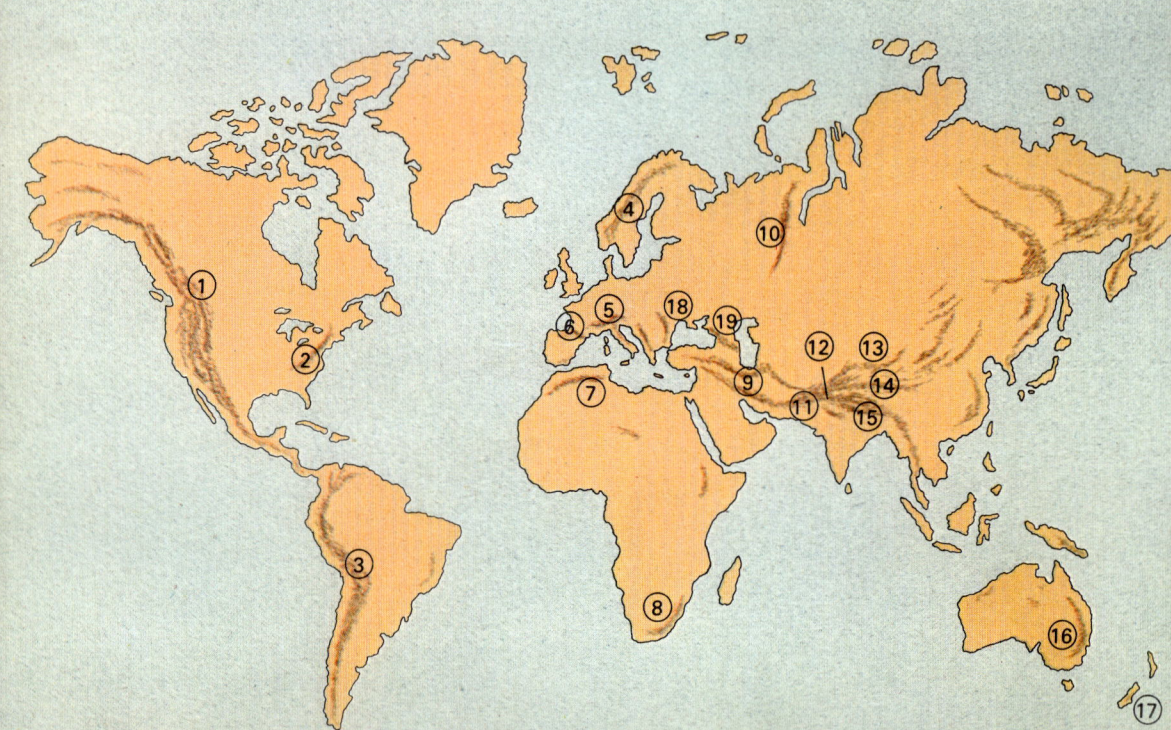

Glossary

Here is a list of some of the special words used in this book.

Adret: the sun-facing side of a valley.

Alpine pasture: the high-level grassland on mountainsides where animals are taken for spring and summer grazing.

Chinook: the warm wind which blows on to the prairies from the Rockies.

Core: the centre of the Earth. The inner core is believed to be solid. The outer core is liquid. Approximate diameter of the core is 6,920 km.

Crust: The Earth's outer layer. Its average depth is about 25 km.

Deciduous trees: trees which shed their leaves in winter.

Delta: an area of flat land at the mouth of a river, made up of silt deposited there by the river.

Erosion: the natural wearing away of the land.

Faults: the fractures, or cracks, in rocks along which the rocks have been displaced by movement in the Earth's crust.

Fjords: a steep-sided valley worn out by a glacier and flooded by the sea.

Föhn: a warm wind blowing down into some Alpine valleys.

Fold: folding, like faulting, is caused by movement in the Earth's surface, but instead of cracking the rocks bend.

Glacier: a mass of ice which flows down a valley.

Hemisphere: half the Earth's surface. The Equator divides the Earth into the northern and southern hemispheres.

Horst: a flattish mountain formed when a block of land is raised up between faults. Large horsts are called block mountains.

Inselbergen: isolated mountains left after the land between them has been worn down to a plain.

Intermontane plateau: a plateau situated between two high mountain ranges.

Magma: very hot liquid rock.

Mantle: the part of the Earth situated beneath the crust and the core. Approximately 2,900 km deep.

Meltwater: water from melted snow or ice.

Mesas and buttes: the isolated remains of eroded plateaux.

Peneplains: these are formed when mountains are eroded into flattish plains.

Plate: the sections of the Earth's crust. Their slow but continuous movement causes changes in the Earth's surface.

Rain shadow: the sheltered or leeward, side of a mountain range where there is less rainfall than on the other, or windward, side.

Rift valley: a steep-sided valley formed when a block of land slips down between two faults.

Scree: the rock fragments which have accumulated at the bottoms of steep mountain slopes.

Sediment: rock fragments ground down into fine grains by river erosion and deposited on to a sea or lake bed.

Sedimentary rock: a rock composed mainly of worn fragments of other rocks. Also rocks such as coal which were formed from once living matter, and rocks formed by chemical action such as rock salt which is left behind when seas dry up.

Snow line: the line on a mountain side above which there is always snow.

Transhumance: the name given to the movement of animals up to the mountain pasture when the snow has melted in the spring and their return to the sheltered valleys in winter.

Ubac: the shady side of a valley.

Windward: the side of a hill facing the wind.

Index